# Start Writing About Things I Do

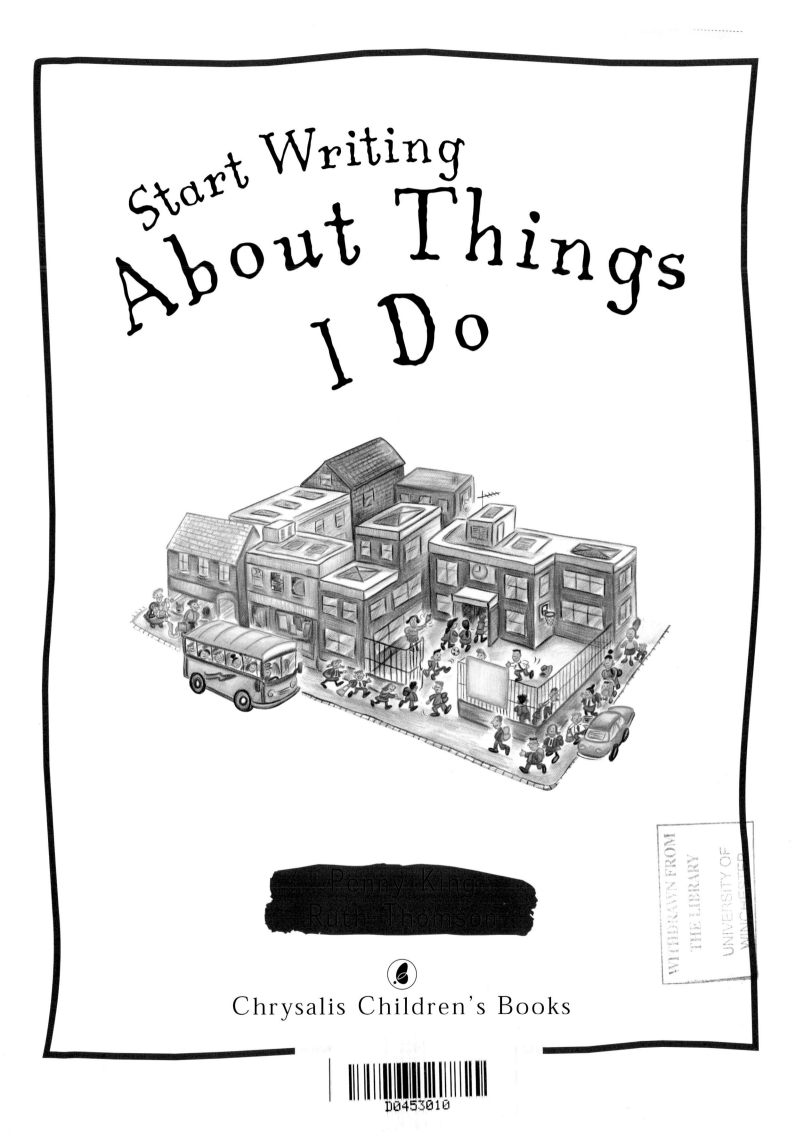

Penny King
Ruth Thomson

🦋

## Chrysalis Children's Books

First published in the UK in 2000 by

Chrysalis Children's Books
64 Brewery Rd, London, N7 9NT

A Belitha Book

ISBN 1 84138 206 X (hardback)
ISBN 1 84138 213 2 (paperback)

British Library in Publication Data for this book
is available from the British Library.

Series editors: Mary-Jane Wilkins, Stephanie Turnbull
Designers: Rachel Hamdi, Holly Mann, Angie Allison
Illustrators: Beccy Blake, Kevin McAleenan, Melanie Mansfield,
   Lisa Smith, Sara Walker
Educational consultants: Pie Corbett, Poet and Consultant
   to the National Literacy Strategy; Sarah Mullen, Literacy Consultant

Printed in Hong Kong

Paperback 10 9 8 7 6 5 4 3
Hardback 10 9 8 7 6 5 4 3 2 1

# Contents

# HOW TO USE THIS BOOK

Can you write a letter, a party invitation or a menu? This book shows you how.

Each double page shows you a different style of writing, such as a menu (shown here). On the left-hand side is an example of the type of writing. On this page it is a menu from a pizza parlour.

Sometimes the writing has labels around it to make it clearer.

On the right-hand page are some ideas for creating your own piece of writing. You can choose one of the suggestions or think of something completely different.

A marvellous menu might include these dishes:

## OUT TO LUNCH

Do you find it hard to choose what to eat in a restaurant? Menus are written to make the food seem delicious and tempting.

So this is the Strawberry Surprise!

### Penny's Pizza Parlour

**Main Courses**

Pizza with ham and juicy pineapple

Pizza with garlic mushrooms, red peppers and sweetcorn

Pizza with spicy sausage and crispy bacon

**Puddings**

Hot apple pie with vanilla ice cream
Strawberry Surprise
Chocolate brownie with fudge sauce

**Drinks**

Freshly-squeezed orange juice
Fizzy lemon
Banana milkshake

Golden drumsticks with melt-in-the-mouth mashed potato

Tagliatelle covered in tangy tomato sauce

Scrumptious strawberry sponge cake

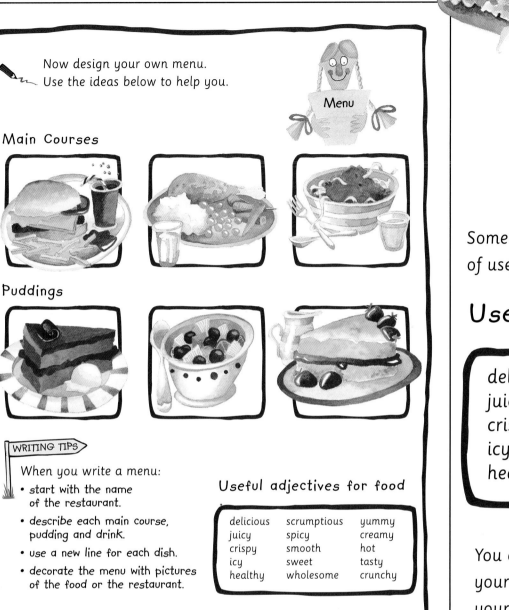

Now design your own menu.
Use the ideas below to help you.

Menu

## Main Courses

## Puddings

WRITING TIPS

When you write a menu:

- start with the name of the restaurant.
- describe each main course, pudding and drink.
- use a new line for each dish.
- decorate the menu with pictures of the food or the restaurant.

### Useful adjectives for food

| | | |
|---|---|---|
| delicious | scrumptious | yummy |
| juicy | spicy | creamy |
| crispy | smooth | hot |
| icy | sweet | tasty |
| healthy | wholesome | crunchy |

Some pages have a box of useful words like this:

## Useful adjectives for food

| | | |
|---|---|---|
| delicious | scrumptious | yummy |
| juicy | spicy | creamy |
| crispy | smooth | hot |
| icy | sweet | tasty |
| healthy | wholesome | crunchy |

You can use these to check your spellings as well as to make your writing more interesting. They are only suggestions! You will probably think of other words you could use.

The writing next to the pencil tells you what to do. Read this through before you start.

WRITING TIPS

The writing tips remind you of things you may need to think about.

# CHOOSING A PET

Have you ever wished you could keep an unusual pet?

Try making a chart comparing some good and bad things about it before you decide.

| Alligators are good pets because... | Alligators are bad pets because... |
|---|---|
| • baby ones are very small. <br> • they don't need exercise. <br> • they can swim in the bath. <br> • they are very quiet. | • they grow very big. <br> • they scare the neighbours. <br> • they sometimes eat people. <br> • they are not very cuddly. <br> • they knock things over. <br> • they can be grumpy. <br> • they don't play. |

I decided that alligators are bad pets because they're not friendly enough.

 Write some good and bad things about keeping a spider or a cat.

## A spider

## A cat

**WRITING TIPS**

Divide your page into two columns with a ruled line.

Write this at the top of the left-hand column.

Write this at the top of the right-hand column.

| Spiders are good pets because... | Spiders are bad pets because... |
|---|---|
| | • they might scare people. |
| | • they are easy to lose. |
| | • |

Write each reason on a new line.

Start each new reason with a bullet point.

Write a final sentence that begins like this or like this.

I decided that spiders are good pets because...

I decided that spiders are bad pets because...

7

# PARTY TIME

Invitations use only a few words, but they tell you everything you need to know about an event.

The name of the party giver

The name of the guest

The kind of party

The place

The date

The time

The clothes to wear

The person who wants your reply (RSVP is short for the French words 'respondez s'il vous plaît' which mean please reply.)

**The King and Queen**

*invite*

**the Ugly Sisters**

*to a ball.*

**at** The Royal Palace
**on** Saturday 8 April
**from** 8 pm to 1 am
**Dress** Ball gowns or uniforms

*RSVP The King and Queen* **Telephone** 00 33 789

The telephone number or address of the party giver

The name on the top line

*The Ugly Sisters*
*Woodland Cottage*
*Forest Road*
*Near Crownsville*
*Fairyland*

The stamp in the top right-hand corner

Each part of the address on a separate line

Write an invitation for one of these parties.
Decorate it to suit the theme of the party.

A barbecue

A fancy-dress birthday party

A princess' christening

# WANTED!

How would you catch a big, bad wolf?
One way is to design a WANTED poster like this.

A title in big letters

# WANTED!
## Big, bad wolf wanted for eating granny.

A picture of the wanted person

Where the person was last seen

Last seen in the dark woods with little Red Riding Hood, wearing a flowery nightdress and fluffy slippers.

How much the reward is

# REWARD £500

If you see the wolf, do not talk to him. Call the police at once.

A warning

Design a WANTED poster
to catch one of these baddies.
Make it bold and clear.

**WRITING TIPS**

When you write your poster:

- put the title – WANTED – at the top.
- describe the baddy and say why he or she is wanted.
- draw a picture of the baddy.
- say where the baddy was last seen.
- say what the reward is.
- tell people what do if they spot the baddy.

## Goldilocks

Wanted for damaging property.

## Hairy Troll

Wanted for threatening goats.

## Jack (with his beanstalk)

Wanted for stealing a giant's hen.

# READY FOR WORK

What clothes do cooks wear? What equipment do they use?
One way of showing this information is to draw a labelled picture.

## EVERYTHING A COOK NEEDS

chopping board

chef's hat

egg whisk

sharp knife

oven gloves

frying pan

colander

apron

tea towel

sieve

cheese grater

scales

mixing bowl

wooden spoon

saucepan

Draw one of these people in working clothes.
Draw any equipment separately and label everything.
There are some suggestions in the boxes below.

## Racing Driver

| | | |
|---|---|---|
| crash helmet | car | gloves |
| wheels | bonnet | tyres |
| seat | wheel | number |

## Clown

| | | |
|---|---|---|
| bow tie | trousers | wig |
| custard pie | bucket | hoop |
| false nose | skittle | make-up |

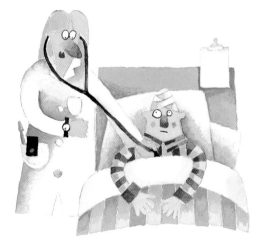

## Doctor

| | | |
|---|---|---|
| stethoscope | bed | chart |
| bleeper | pen | bandage |
| thermometer | watch | white coat |

## Monster Hunter

| | | |
|---|---|---|
| helmet | boots | camera |
| water bottle | rucksack | hat |
| binoculars | net | notebook |

# ABOUT TOWN

How would you describe a building?

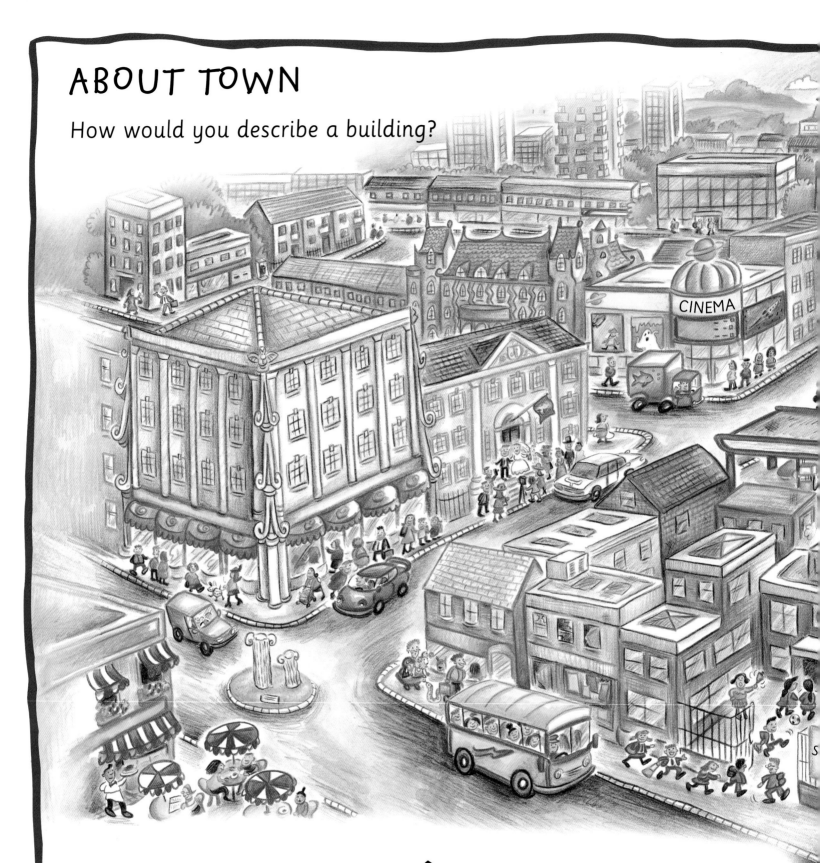

CINEMA

This is a description of a building in the picture above. Which one?

This new building is in the centre of town.
It has big posters on the walls outside.
People come here to see films.
It is very busy on Saturday nights.

Choose another building.

Say where it is, what it looks like and what goes on there. Do not give its name. Ask a friend to guess what it is.

When you describe a building:

- write in the present tense.
- use one or more of these helpful adjectives.

| old | ancient | new | modern |
| tall | small | huge | low |
| high | square | round | twisted |
| round | grand | smart | shabby |

- say where the building is.
- point out one of its features. For example, does it have lots of windows or a sign outside?
- say why people go there.
- think of an interesting fact about it.

# OUT TO LUNCH

Do you find it hard to choose what to eat in a restaurant? Menus are written to make the food seem delicious and tempting.

So this is the Strawberry Surprise!

## Penny's Pizza Parlour

### Main Courses

Pizza with ham and juicy pineapple

Pizza with garlic mushrooms, red peppers and sweetcorn

Pizza with spicy sausage and crispy bacon

### Puddings

Hot apple pie with vanilla ice cream

Strawberry Surprise

Chocolate brownie with fudge sauce

### Drinks

Freshly-squeezed orange juice

Fizzy lemon

Banana milkshake

Now design your own menu.
Use the ideas below to help you.

Menu

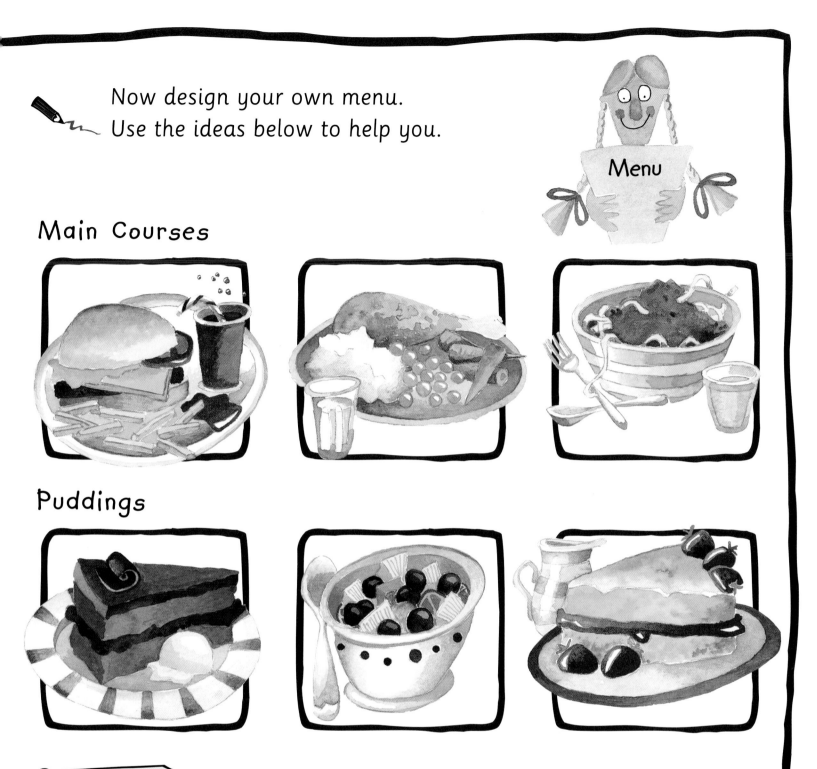

## Main Courses

## Puddings

> WRITING TIPS

When you write a menu:

- start with the name of the restaurant.

- describe each main course, pudding and drink.

- use a new line for each dish.

- decorate the menu with pictures of the food or the restaurant.

## Useful adjectives for food

| | | |
|---|---|---|
| delicious | scrumptious | yummy |
| juicy | spicy | creamy |
| crispy | smooth | hot |
| icy | sweet | tasty |
| healthy | wholesome | crunchy |

# SCHOOL RULES

Schools have rules to keep everyone safe and happy.

Ziggle's class made this list of rules for their playground. Which rules are being ignored?

## Playground Rules

1. Keep your suckers to yourself.
2. Treat all aliens kindly.
3. Line up sensibly.
4. Leave your dangerous pets at home.
5. Put space snack wrappers in the bin.
6. Take turns to play on the Twisty Tower.
7. Watch where you are flying.
8. Don't climb on the school walls.
9. Don't fight with lasers.
10. Make sure the playground is empty before you land your space pod.

What rules would you make for this playground?

Write a list of ten rules. Use the picture to help you. Number each rule and begin it with a bossy verb.

## Bossy verbs

| | | |
|---|---|---|
| don't | try | put |
| take turns | watch | line up |
| go | play | help |
| share | look | pick up |
| listen | make sure | ask |

# MY NEWS

Do you enjoy telling people your news? Billy wrote about his birthday, starting in the morning and ending in the evening.

1.

2.

3.

4.

On Saturday it was my sixth birthday. After breakfast I had my present. It was a racing bike. Then Mum, Dad, Sam and I went to the park. First I rode my bike. I wobbled a lot! Next we hired a boat. I paddled but I soon got tired. Later Granny came for a special meal. My cake was a dinosaur shape. It was my best birthday ever.

This is what Suzy and her brother Matt did on Saturday.
Imagine you are Suzy or Matt and write a recount of the day.

1.

2.

3.

4.

WRITING TIPS

- Begin your account by saying when it happened.

- Say who was with you.

- Tell your reader where you went.

- Say what you did.

- When you have finished, make a comment about your day.

- Remember to use useful words about time.

| first | next | soon |
| later | afterwards | before |
| finally | then | at last |

# HIT THE HEADLINES

Does your family read a newspaper?

Imagine if the story of the Queen of Hearts was on the front page. It might look like this.

> The Queen of Hearts made some tarts
> All on a summer's day.
> The Knave of Hearts stole those tarts
> and took them clean away.

The name of the newspaper

A short headline

Who the story is about

The name of the writer

## THE DAILY NEWS

# QUEEN'S TARTS STOLEN!

By Ivana Deer

A picture of someone in the story

The sad queen in her kitchen.

A caption that tells readers about the picture

What happened

When it happened

Where it happened

Police are still hunting for the Knave of Hearts. He is suspected of stealing the Queen's jam tarts yesterday afternoon. All harbours and airports are being watched in case he tries to escape abroad.

The police went to the Palace this morning to interview the unhappy Queen, aged 35.

She said, 'I left the tarts by the window to cool. When I came back, they had vanished. I saw the Knave running away in the distance.'

The Queen had made the tarts as a surprise for the King's birthday. People from all over the country have sent her hundreds of new tarts.

Retell one of these nursery rhymes as a front page newspaper story.

Hey, diddle diddle.
The cat and the fiddle.
The cow jumped over the moon.
The little dog laughed to see such fun
And the dish ran away with the spoon.

Mary had a little lamb
Its fleece was white as snow.
And everywhere that Mary went
That lamb was sure to go.
It followed her to school one day
That was against the rules.
It made the children laugh and play
To see the lamb at school.

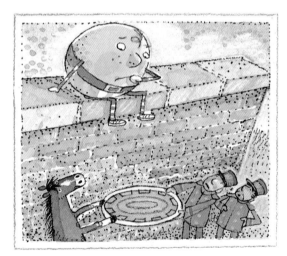

Humpty Dumpty sat on a wall.
Humpty Dumpty had a great fall.
All the King's horses
And all the King's men
Couldn't put Humpty together again.

WRITING TIPS

When you write your newspaper report, make sure you say:

- who it is about.
- what happened.
- when it happened.
- where it happened.
- why it happened (if you know).

# GOOD ENOUGH TO EAT

Recipes start with a list of ingredients. They describe how to use the ingredients (the method) and how long it takes to make (the preparation time).

## GIANT EGG ROLLS

## Ingredients

- 1 extra-large French stick
- 500g butter
- 12 hard-boiled eggs
- 6 tablespoons mayonnaise
- salt and pepper
- 2 lettuces

## Method

1. Peel the hard-boiled eggs. Mash them in a bowl with a fork. Add salt and pepper. Stir in the mayonnaise.

2. Cut the French stick in half. Spread butter on both halves.

3. Wash the lettuces and shred them.

4. Spread the egg mixture on the bottom half of the French stick.

5. Cover it with the shredded lettuce.

6. Finally, put the other half of the French stick on top.

## Preparation time

15–20 minutes

This recipe is very popular with giants in summertime.

Invent a revolting recipe to delight a dreadful dragon.

## Some ideas for ingredients

rotten eggs

prickly thistles

mouldy bread

wiggly worms

a plump princess

a fat frog

sour grapes

tomato ketchup

double cream

nettles

a string of sausages

fish bones

hot chillies

## Useful verbs

| add | spread | cut | chop |
| fill | stir | slice | mix |
| bake | pour | put | whisk |
| boil | fry | crush | mash |

I'm starving. Where's my lunch?

**WRITING TIPS**

When you write a recipe:

- think of a name for it.
- list the ingredients.
- say how much you need of each one.
- describe the method. Make sure you include every ingredient.
- say what must be done first, next and last.
- number the steps.
- say how long the recipe takes to make.
- at the end, say something interesting about your recipe.

# AMAZING ADVERTS

Advertisements are designed to catch your eye. They try to make you desperate for the thing they advertise.

## Roly Poly Coaster

Go Round the Bend!

DO YOU DARE
to whizz, loop
and twist
on
a journey
of terror?

Only 2 minutes walk from the entrance.
Parents go free!

Write an advert for another ride. Use a few words, clear writing and bright colours.

## Useful verbs

| | | | |
|---|---|---|---|
| whirr | grind | fly | creak |
| crash | wail | splash | scream |
| fall | roll | climb | plunge |
| twist | roar | bounce | spin |

WRITING TIPS

When you write your advert:

- think of a short, catchy name for the ride.

- ask questions starting with things like:

    Do you dare...?
    Are you brave enough for...?

- include some verbs to describe what the ride does.

- describe where the ride is.

- remember – people always like something free!

# FAN LETTERS

Letters are great fun to send and receive.
When you write a letter remember these things.

Write your address in the top right-hand corner.

Always begin with the word Dear.

25 Castle View
Moatstown
Knights Bridge
KN5 2MN

3 November 2000

Write today's date under the address.

Dear Ms Cox,

Use the person's title and surname.

I am writing to tell you how much I loved your book, The Dragon's Dinner. I was given it for my birthday.

Say why you are writing.

It was so funny when you wrote about the dragon becoming a vegetarian! We all cried when his mother left him in the zoo because he was so greedy.

Do you use a computer or a pen for writing? It is Book Week soon at our school and we wondered if you could come and talk to us about how you write your books. We have lots of questions we would like to ask you.

Ask questions – it is a good way to get a reply!

Look on page 8 to find out how to address an envelope.

With best wishes,

Anna Wheeler
(aged 7)

Write your name and age clearly.

28

Is there someone you really admire?

Surprise them with a fan letter.
Cross your fingers for a reply!

Your favourite sports personality

Your favourite
band or singer

WRITING TIPS

- Put some lined paper under your writing paper for really straight lines.

- Here are some different ways to end your letters:

| Yours | Lots of love |
| Yours sincerely | With best wishes |
| Love from | Write soon |

Your favourite writer

# LIFE STORIES

The explanation below tells you how sunflowers grow from seeds.

## The Life Story of a Sunflower

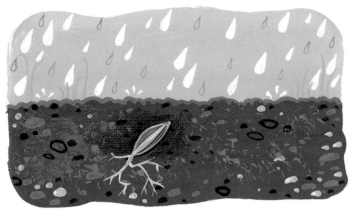

1. The seed swells in warm, wet, spring weather. The roots push down into the soil.

2. A few weeks later, a shoot appears. The roots keep growing.

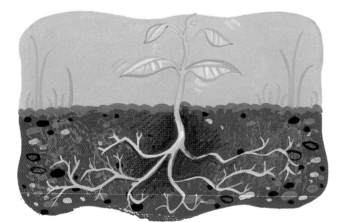

3. Next the leaves start to grow. The plant grows taller and taller.

4. Soon it is taller than a person. A flower bud appears.

5. In summer the bud opens. The flower turns towards the sun.

6. Later seeds form and finally the petals fade and die.

Use these pictures and labels to tell the life story of a frog. Make sure your explanation is in order.

WRITING TIPS

When you write an explanation:

- first think of a title.
- write in the present tense.
- describe what happens in the right order.
- use time words such as first, then, next, after and finally.

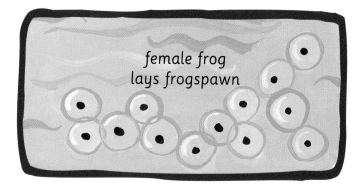

female frog lays frogspawn

1. Spring.

tadpole hatches

2. After 2 weeks.

breathes through gills

gills

3. After 4 weeks.

back legs grow

gills disappear

breathes air

4. After 8 weeks.

tail shortens

front legs grow

5. After 10 weeks.

becomes froglet

6. After 12 weeks.